The DIY Wedding

*An Essential Guide to DIY
Wedding Ideas, Including
Invitations, Decorations,
Centerpieces, Programs,
and Favors*

by **Riva Maestro**

Table of Contents

Introduction

If you're a DIY junkie who's preparing for a dream wedding, then you'll love this book. This is for all you girls that appreciate everything Etsy has to offer, but unfortunately just can't afford to pay for someone else's time. It's also for you girls that can never find "just the perfect thing." This is your opportunity to create your own wedding paraphernalia exactly to your liking.

Each chapter is focused on a separate component of your wedding, from the invitations to the centerpieces to the party favors. And of course, there are different levels of DIY, depending on how in-depth you'd like to get. For example, I'll mention when you can purchase kits or sets that'll give you everything you need and all you have to do is put it together. Or, if you're really artsy-craftsy, I'll fully explain the process so you can make everything from scratch. I'll give you a complete list of required and suggested materials, as well as the step-by-step instructions to create the item at hand. Everything will be super easy and fun to do, and your guests will be astonished when you tell them that you made everything yourself.

Don't wait until the last minute though. Simple and fun though these projects may be, they will take time to perfect, and you want everything to be absolutely flawless on your wedding day. If you need some extra help getting it all done, you might want to think about enlisting your bridal party. This can actually be a fun plan for a low-key bachelorette party or as an awesome way for the bridal party to bond prior to the big day, especially if they haven't all met before.

Just make sure you restrain yourself from making your own wedding dress. I'm not very traditional, but I've heard that's bad luck!

Chapter 1: Wedding Invitations

Your wedding invitations are very important. They're like a first impression, and they set the mood for your wedding. There are so many ways to make a wedding invite that I couldn't possibly tell you all of them. I like to think of these as jumping off points to expand upon if you like them.

Postcard Wedding Invitations

This is one way to give people a traditional paper invitation with an added contemporary flair. This way, you save on money for envelopes. A traditional postcard is rectangular in shape, 3.5 inches by 5 inches. The easiest way to do this yourself would be to design it in Photoshop or any other design based computer software program. This way, you can easily set the proper dimensions you'll need. Pick a dynamic picture to go on it. Because this is a wedding invite, I would suggest an engagement picture. Whatever picture you go with, be sure that you pick something that is high-resolution enough to hold up to printing. To do this effectively, your DPI should be at least 240. One of the major earmarks of a postcard is that it's bold, colorful, and graphic, so keep this in mind when selecting an image.

Set your image and decide whether you would like a border or not. If you do, then use the ruler tool in Photoshop to make sure that it's the correct width and placement. Then use layers to create your graphics. If you're thinking ahead, it'd be a nice tie in to have it be the same font as your place settings and programs.

Don't clutter up the front with more than just your general invite greeting such as: "You are invited to the wedding of (insert name) and (insert name)." Then, either create a back, or handwrite it. If you choose to print it, just be sure that your printer will allow you to do a double-sided document. Of course, if you really want to carry on with the postcard feel, I would hand pen it. Make sure that you include all the relevant information, such as:

- Date

- Time

- Place

- Dress Code

- RSVP

- Whether or not your guest will be bringing a date or other guests

Traditional Cardstock Invitations

To make things easier, use the same template for your programs and your invites if you want to go the more traditional route. You could do either a booklet-like invite or a one-page invite. Refer to Chapter 4 for program instructions, which are going to be similar to the above postcard instructions. Just replace the schedule information with all of the proper event information.

Virtual Invitations

Even though I would always suggest sending out paper invitations (it's classier), it might also be a good idea to send an "evite", because people check their emails more often. There are many services you can choose from, such as: evite.com, greenvelope.com, and punchbowl.com just to name a few. They have plenty of premade, gorgeous templates to choose from, and this way, you can be sure that all your guests receive their invitations.

Chapter 2: Mood-Setting Decorations

I think that the prettiest, most effective decorations for a wedding are those you see in outdoor weddings. Of course, if you happen to be having an indoor wedding, then there are fun things you can do too, but since it's summer, I'm going to be operating under the assumption that most people will be holding their ceremonies, if not their receptions, outdoors.

Hanging Lanterns

This is one of my favorite decorations for any summer party, especially a wedding. You can purchase premade lanterns and place candles inside, make paper lanterns, or tin lanterns.

There are many ways to make a paper lantern, but for this design, you will need:

Any size and weight of paper you want. I would suggest either a matching or complimenting cardstock to your invitations or your programs. The thicker the paper, the better. That way the lantern will hold up.

- Fold your paper in half lengthwise.

- Cut slits perpendicular to the folded edge, but don't completely sever the paper. These are the slits, which are going to allow the light to shine through. The shorter the slit, the sturdier the lantern, but it's up to you. Also decide how far apart you want the slits to be, and ensure that you cut them an equal distance apart

- Once you're done making slits, fold the paper around and glue or tape it together to create your lantern shape. Don't forget to tape it on the inside so it looks neat.

- Choose how you would like to hang your lantern. You can either cut a strip of paper to create a handle and tape or glue it to the inside of the lantern, or you can punch two small holes in the top and attach string. If you plan on placing candles inside your lanterns, you should choose a fairly strong ribbon.

These would look sweet hung from tree branches or porch railings.

- If you would like a candle in your lantern, make sure the candle has glass around it, then place the lantern over the top.

For a tin lantern, you will need:

- A tin can

- Markers

- A nail and hammer

To make it:

- Clean your can and draw whatever pattern you would like on the outside.

- Fill it up with ice to help prevent denting.

- Use the hammer and nail to lightly tap out your patterns.

- Remove the ice and add a wire handle.

These will be much sturdier to place candles inside and hang from trees. If they aren't going to be on a flat surface, you might want to tape or glue the candle onto the base of the lantern so that it's secure.

Daisy Chains

You don't actually have to use daisies; you can use whatever flowers compliment your bouquet.

You will need:

- Flowers. Make sure they still have stems on them.

- Scissors or an exacto knife, depending on what you prefer.

Make a half-inch slit in each daisy stem to start. Pull the stem of the next flower through the slit in the first one. Basically, you're just going to repeat this process until you have the length you want. Typically, when you're done, you would link the final flower to the first one. But for this, I would suggest linking each end of the chain to a strong length of rope or ribbon, whichever best fits your aesthetics. Then you could hang them from trees, porch railings, or the backs of chairs for your ceremony. I find this much softer and more feminine than flag garlands.

Chapter 3: Table Decorations and Centerpieces

Tea Lights

Tea lights are a good basic decoration that every wedding should have, especially if the festivities are going to continue past dark. If you're worried about a fire hazard, there are battery powered tea lights available as well. These can be placed on tables among strewn rose petals or other available petals as a table decoration all by themselves, or as an addition to another centerpiece. If you don't have, or can't afford, rose petals, you could use any seasonal flower or dried flower. If it's fall, and the leaves are still fresh, it could be a lovely idea.

Traditional Centerpiece: Bud Vases

Any traditional centerpiece, to me, would be anything with a flower arrangement. If you can't afford a large profusion of flowers, just one bud vase would be fine. In fact, if you feel that the table would look too crowded with both a centerpiece and place settings, then just use a singular bud vase for each place setting. Again, it might be a good idea to tie it back into your wedding by using the same flowers as the spray from your bouquet. Sprays is less expensive, but just as pretty.

Quirky Statue Place Settings

If you only care whether people sit at the correct table and not necessarily whom they sit by, you could denote each table by a quirky little sculpture. They could be pretty wire trees in different colors or little figurines you can pick up at Goodwill. Again, if you have a lot of children in attendance, it might be cool to pick up some of the paintable statues that are sold at craft stores, along with paint. Give each guest one with a place number or name card.

Floral Centerpiece Ideas

A floral centerpiece is a pretty standard wedding idea, but there are many ways it can be interpreted. If you want something larger than just bud vases, here are a few ideas:

- Use milk bottles or other glass bottles banded together with twine or ribbon. You can use all the same shape or create dimension by gathering larger bottles in the middle and working outward to smaller bottles.

- Use cake platters to place flowers on. You can make a flower ball by cutting a floral foam ball in half so that it sits flat, soaking it, and then inserting the flower stems into the foam. If you have smaller flowers you'd rather use or you don't like the idea of a circular ball of flowers, you could get a cake platter with a dome, fill up the cake platter, then place the dome on top.

Chapter 4: Programs for the Ceremony

Programs are relatively simple and easy to make. Generally, a wedding program should not run longer than one page in length. You don't want to overwhelm your guests with things to do. Here are a few of my favorite ideas for wedding programs. Make sure that you alter them so that they match the theme of your wedding.

Interactive Programs

In the next chapter, a lot of my party favor ideas are interactive so that your guests have a chance to customize their goodie bags. If you would like to continue on in this vein, then you can create what I like to call an interactive program. There are two ways you can go about doing this.

The first is to create a spinning wheel, like a prize wheel at a fair. This can work especially well if you have a carnival like theme, and a fairly free-flowing schedule. It's also fun if you happen to have a lot of small children in attendance. What you can do is create a giant pinwheel from cardboard. Using old packing boxes and spray paint will do, just make it pretty. After it's decorated, label it with different events that will happen at the wedding reception. This can include things like: cake cutting, dinner service, guest book signing, gift unwrapping, first dance, any speeches that need to be made, or party games you plan on playing. After the wedding, when it's time to begin the festivities, allow one of the children in attendance to spin the wheel, thus selecting the order in which you do things.

If you don't feel like going through all the trouble of making a giant pinwheel, you could always write the options on strips of paper and allow the guests to draw each one out, one at a time.

Traditional Programs

Traditional programs have one page, but they also have a front and a back. The actual information is sandwiched between a glossy, cardstock that has your wedding monogram on it. It's simple, traditional, and above all, denotes classic elegance. Pick a heavy cardstock in a color that goes well with your wedding. Cut it to the size you want. This is where you can get a bit non-traditional if you want, because you can make it a traditional 8.5x11 hamburger fold size, or it could be rectangular, square, or really any other shape you want.

Whether you choose a funky shape or not, to get the best results, it's a good idea to put your design, shape, dimensions and all the components, like your logo and information list into Photoshop or a similar program to make sure everything meshes together smoothly. Unless you have excellent calligraphy and cutting skills, things will look off if you do it entirely by hand. Design and plan out the monogram to go on the front cover. This may be the part that you want to hire someone else to do, unless you are a graphic designer or artist yourself. Use the Photoshop line guides to make sure everything is properly lined up.

You'll want the front and plain back to be thick cardstock, but you'll also need to design and print out a thinner piece of paper to be glued on the inside, this will be your actual program of events. While you can use plain computer paper if needed, I would suggest looking in the scrapbooking section of your local crafts store for some awesome printmaking or tissue-like paper. Just make sure that it's thick enough to run through the printer. However, if you have access to a professional, photo-grade printer, you should be good to go. Pick a font for the schedule that is beautiful and elegant, but also readable.

After you've got everything printed out, line up your cardstock to hole punch it. You might want to do a nice, good-sized punch so that you can thread through a thick, luxurious silk or velvet ribbon. Paste your schedule onto the back piece of cardstock and allow it to thoroughly dry before you attach the front monogrammed piece. And you're finished!

Program Fans—Version One

Either version of these is perfect for a summer wedding. This first is just a simple paddle fan. All you need is some extra thick cardstock (like the consistency of cardboard), and Popsicle sticks. You can either print your schedule onto the cardstock directly, (unless it's too thick to go through a printer) or print it onto a thinner paper and paste it onto the paddle fan. After it's dry, attach the Popsicle stick and you're in business.

Program Fans—Version Two

In my opinion, this version is much more elegant, but it does require a bit more work. This is a folding fan style. You can either fan-fold your paper yourself from cardstock, then attach Popsicle sticks as supporting spines, or you can purchase pre-made fans. It's really up to you, your experience level, and how much time you have.

Either way, onto the fans, you'll write the order of events into the folds in a contrasting color of pen. If you don't have pretty handwriting, make sure you ask someone that does to do it. You want your programs to look neat and consistent, even when it's DIY.

Cootie Catchers

This is a cute idea, especially for those of us born in the late 80s and early 90s. For those of you who don't know what a cootie catcher is, it's a little origami fortune predictor. As kids, we used to write on it different options as answers to questions such as, "Who will I marry one day?" While these particular cootie catchers won't exactly be "functional," they certainly are adorable and will make your guests smile. If you don't know or remember how to make them, here are some quick instructions.

You will need:

- A square piece of paper

- A pen

If your paper isn't already square, you can fold it diagonally and trim off the excess, but I have to say that origami paper works just fine and is much prettier, especially when it comes to wedding programs. Now all you need to do is:

- Decorate one side of your paper. If you draw or paint, feel free to do that, but make it consistent.

- After everything is dry, you should fold it in half lengthwise, making a very firm crease. Then, unfold it again.

- Then, fold widthwise, and again, unfold.

- Fold each corner towards the center of the square. They should line up easily.

- Flip the whole thing over, and repeat the same steps, folding each corner towards the center.

- Then fold the paper in half again in each direction. At this step, no unfolding is necessary.

- Flip your cootie catcher over to its original side, and it should look like four small squares. Pull the tabs towards you and the center should fold in.

- Label the tabs of your cootie catcher: each of the corners gets a color, the inside tabs get the fortune (or in this case the schedule information) and the outside of the inside tabs get labeled with a number.

This is my absolutely favorite program idea.

Hand Painted Programs

If you have a painter among your friends or family, this would be a great idea, and can be applied to any of the above program ideas or to any premade program. The only difference would be that I would suggest using watercolor paper so that your paint doesn't run. You could paint the same scene or monogram on each program, or paint different things. It's a cool way for the artists you know to show off their skills, it's also a unique gift for your guests.

Single Page Programs

I would create these in the exact way as the monogrammed ones, the only difference being that you would print your monogram (if you have one) at the top of your schedule piece. This will save you paper and ink, and you could still hole punch the sides and add a ribbon accent.

Chapter 5: Wedding Favors

I have to say, the favors are my favorite part. Your guests are going to be bringing you the big gifts, like the new bedding set or that stand mixer you've had your eye on for a while now, but the truth is everyone loves gifts; so why not give your guests something sweet (both literally and figuratively) to take home? These are some of my favorite ideas, and if something inspires you and gives you another idea, go for it. Don't limit yourself to only these. The reason I love all of these is because they are gender neutral, everyone can find something they like, and they're all somewhat interactive. Of course, they don't have to be interactive; you can prepackage things, but I think it would be fun to allow people to pack up their own gift bags. It's less work for you, and everyone gets something they would actually use.

Lavender or Other Floral Sachets

I love lavender. Anyone who knows me knows that it's true. And I know that everyone likes their clothes or pillows to smell awesome. Plus, lavender sachets are simple to make and very pretty. If you grow your own lavender or other fragrant flowers, such as rose hip or lilies or marigold (basically anything that smells awesome), you might want to start picking and drying them. If you don't have a green thumb (or if it's the wrong time of year) you can order dried flowers inexpensively online, or check with your local flower shop. You'll also need some linen, lightweight cotton, or pure silk to make the sachets from. You can also purchase drawstring bags if you don't want to make them.

If you want to pre-make the bags to put in gift bags or next to place settings, you can go ahead and do that. But if you decide to go the interactive route, you could set up a station with trays of the different flowers and allow your guests to make up their custom sachets.

Tiny Terrariums or Succulents

Terrariums are so simple that even children can make them. Whether you choose to give pre-potted succulents or to make terrariums is going to be based on how creative you think your guests are. In any case, you're going to need to purchase succulents. If you choose to make, or allow your guests to make, terrariums, you will need:

- Clear glass vases or vessels. They can be any color, size, or shape you want, and don't all have to be the same

- Succulents and cacti of varying sizes

- Pebbles to hold the succulents in

- Sand, for the same purpose

- Plant food that's specifically for cacti and succulents

Into the vessel, you're going to layer up your plant food, pebbles and then sand on top. Depress the area that you want to plant with your fingers, and create a hole just big enough for the plant. Starting with bigger plants is best, because you can group smaller plants around them and make cool landscaping decisions. Leave about an inch of space around each plant to allow room for growth. Layer a little bit more sand and pebbles on top to make it pretty.

If you decide to allow your guests to do this themselves, it might be a good idea to attach a homemade instructions card to each empty vessel so that when they go up to the station they know exactly what to do. Either way, whether you choose to give your guests succulents or terrariums, you should attach an instructions card telling them to give it water once every one or two weeks, or whenever the soil gets dry. Also advise them to give the plants direct sunlight every day. The homemade instructions cards can just be little pieces of cardstock attached to the vessel with ribbon or raffia.

Candy Stand

This is a super cute and fun idea for guests of all ages. Depending on the budget of your wedding, you could either go to the store and buy basic candies that everyone will enjoy, or you could get specialty candies made. If you don't have a local shop you can purchase from, look online. There are all sorts of specialty candy shops. If your wedding has a particular theme, you should choose the candy to match it. This is also true if you have specific wedding colors. If your wedding is happening around the same time as a major holiday, you could have specific flavors made to correspond to it. Aside from things like chocolate and lollipops, you could include all sorts of cookies. If you choose to include the cookies, make sure to put each kind in a separate container and to clearly label them so that guests with food allergies will be aware of what they might be picking up. Decorate a table and set everything out complete with boxes and bags for guests to put their choices in.

Custom Tea Mix

I've seen this as a party favor at weddings before, but now I'd like to add my own twist. If you've ever been to Teavana or similar stores, you know that they keep their tea in large jars and they have many premixed flavors. If you are satisfied with the premixed flavors go ahead with that, but it might also be an idea to ask about creating your own flavor that's unique to your wedding. One of my favorite sites to create unique teas is called Adagio.com. On Adagio, they have a section that's specifically for creating a unique tea blend. There's a how to video, and you can either select a "popular blend formation," as they call it, or pick three base teas to create your own. First, you select the tea type, then select the percentage that you would like each tea type to have in your blend. An idea on how to select your flavors could be to have it emulate your wedding cake flavor. Then, you get to name it, describe it, and tell others why you created the blend. The blend can then be saved on the site for others to purchase later. If you really love your guests, get each of them a bag. If you don't have that much money to go around, just buy a few bags and split them into smaller portions, like a cute little tin. Set them out next to the place settings or put them into gift bags.

Honey or Jam

Everybody loves homemade food, especially honey and jam. After all, you can put them on anything. If you aren't particularly good at cooking and you don't know anyone that can make jam (or teach you how to make jam) you might want to go with the honey. Local honey is especially good, since it can help to prevent allergies if you eat it everyday. If you want to make your honey unique, you can infuse it. Here's a quick instruction on how to infuse honey. You will need:

- Honey (again, I always prefer local)

- Herbs, spices, or fruit zest (think of flavors you like, or taste the honey to find flavors that would complement its base flavor)

- Tea bags

- Double boiler or large pot

- Small canning jars

- A grater (if you've chosen to use fruit zest)

- Knife, cutting board, and measuring cups

You'll need to stick your jars and lids into your pot or boiler and boil them for about ten minutes to sterilize them. If you choose to make jam, you'll also do this. While your jars are boiling, you should rinse and dry the ingredients you plan to use in your infusion. Some of the things you might choose to infuse your honey with are: orange zest, rosemary, thyme, mint, lemon zest, or my favorite, which is a combination of cardamom pods, cinnamon sticks, and ginger. Try infusing a small batch of honey first to figure out what proportions you prefer.

Though I've made infused honey with loose herbs and spices before, it can be a bit of a pain. (Except with the cinnamon sticks, which is best to leave whole). You can purchase empty tea bags and fill them up with your spices and zest to make things a little bit easier.

Once you have your zest prepared, you're going to set up the double boiler (or the larger pot with a smaller, heat resistant glass bowl inside), with your desired amount of honey. Normally half a cup is sufficient, especially for the one-person servings you are going to give out at your wedding. Add your teabag. Let the teabag steep in the honey at about 185 degrees Fahrenheit for about ten minutes. Allow to cool for about the same amount of time before removing the teabag and jarring. The honey would be a perfect compliment to specialized tea!

On to the jam. You will need:

- 4 cups of fresh fruit of your choice— personally I prefer cherry and strawberry jams, but you can also use apricot, grape, or any other type of seasonal berry—and if it's fall or winter and you still want to make jam, frozen fruit from summer or the grocery store works just as well

- One packet of pectin

- 4 cups of sugar—it could be more or less, based on personal taste

- ¼ cup lemon juice

- ½ teaspoon butter, or butter substitute if preferred

Sterilize the jars you're going to use for jarring in the same way as for the honey. Prepare your fruit. This includes any washing, pitting, coring or stem removal that might be necessary. If you're using larger fruits, cut them up. There's no need to do any fine dicing; sizeable chunks will do.

Crush the fruit up to make it more manageable. If you prefer smooth jelly over jam, you're going to be crushing it up for a while, and in this case, I might even use a meat pulverizer to make things a little bit easier.

In a saucepan, combine the fruit, lemon, and butter. Bring the mixture to a rolling boil while stirring constantly to make sure it doesn't stick. Pour in the sugar until it dissolves completely. If you use less than a 1:2 sugar to fruit ratio, your jam may be a bit runny. However, if you do have the time to make a few batches before you make the batch for your wedding, I would suggest doing so, so that you can find your desired consistency and sweetness.

Let the jelly simmer on low heat. The optimal time could be anywhere between five and thirty minutes, depending on the type of fruit and your desired consistency. When your jam is ready, remove it from the heat, and skim off any bubbles that might remain on top. Don't worry, that happens naturally and won't hurt anything, but it will affect the flavor if you don't remove them. Then spoon the finished jelly into the jars and prepare the tops to your jars. To do this, you need to boil your jar seals in a small amount of water until they soften. Then they are ready to be put onto your jars. Most jars that you buy will come with more detailed instructions on how to do this. Then you have to boil the jars again with the jam inside, for about ten minutes. Lift them out with tongs so you don't burn yourself.

And you're finished. All these party favors are practical, useful, or edible, and are all gender neutral. No matter the theme or color of your wedding, you can dress it up in cute jars with little name cards to make them match.

Conclusion

I hope that this little book has given you plenty of ideas for your summer DIY wedding. From lovely rustic centerpieces to interactive candy stations and lavender sachets, from handmade invitations and programs to tea lights and hanging lanterns, it should cover all the basics. If you buy DIYs from someone else, it can cost a lot of money because of the time and effort involved in making them. But if you choose to do it yourself, you can benefit from the savings and take credit.

Making all the accoutrements for your wedding is a great way for members of your wedding party to interact and get to know one another. And if enough members of your wedding party or guest list are impressed, you might even choose to hand out little cards with complete instructions to some of the items you've made. That way, any other brides-to-be can also benefit from the savings.

Even though it will be cheaper, making most of your decorations and paper goods is going to take time, so make sure you plan for it, and give yourself plenty of time to make mistakes and choose to make a variation if you like one look or flavor better than the other. Also work out a budget to make sure you're actually saving yourself some money.

As you choose what items to make, be sure to personalize them to match your wedding, either with a specialized logo or theme, or with your wedding colors or flowers. No matter which items from this book you choose to make, the most important thing is to make your wedding easier on yourself, and to have fun while doing so.

Finally, I'd like to thank you for purchasing this book! If you enjoyed it or found it helpful, I'd greatly appreciate it if you'd take a moment to leave a review on Amazon. Thank you!

39070693R00030

Made in the USA
San Bernardino, CA
20 September 2016